Till Day
You Do
Part

PETER HANDKE

Till Day You Do Part
Or, A Question of Light

TRANSLATED BY MIKE MITCHELL

LONDON NEW YORK CALCUTTA

 **GOETHE INSTITUT**

This publication was supported by a
grant from the Goethe-Institut India

Seagull Books, 2019

Originally published in German as Peter Handke, *Bis daß der Tag
euch scheidet oder Eine Frage des Lichts*: *Ein Monolog*

German original © Suhrkamp Verlag, Frankfurt am Main 2009

English translation © Mike Mitchell, 2010

First published in English translation by Seagull Books, 2010

Second printing, 2019

ISBN 978 0 8574 2 530 0

British Library Cataloguing-in-Publication Data
A catalogue record for this book is available from the British Library

Typeset by Seagull Books, Calcutta, India
Printed and bound by WordsWorth India, New Delhi, India

For S

CONTENTS

TILL DAY YOU DO PART

OR, A QUESTION OF LIGHT

What's that I can see? Doesn't it look like a gravestone, the kind they used to have for Roman couples, man and wife beside each other, as if carved out of stone?—only that's not just the two heads, they're whole figures, a couple moreover, life-size and detached from the shared stone or whatever it is—not reliefs but complete sculptures or figures, each standing upright in its niche, each close to the other, even if not at all monumental. The clothing and faces are of the same greyish white as the stone box or whatever it is surrounding them. Their eyes are greyish white as well, closed in both cases. Both statues or figures have the same posture, their heads facing forward.

And yet if we look long enough a difference between the two, beyond the usual ones

between a man and a woman, does strike us.
Although as upright as the woman beside him,
the man, with not only sunken and wrinkled
cheeks but a similar mouth and very concave
temples into the bargain, looks as dead and
gone as anyone can. It makes no difference that
someone, perhaps a drunk on his way home,
has painted his lips a deep red, stuck a red
cardboard nose on him and wrapped stuff that
looks like bits of tape from a cassette round his
forehead.
By contrast, despite her chalky colour, the
statue of the woman looks—how should I put
it?—bursting with life. That comes first of all
from her lips, pursed in an enigmatic smile,
such as you only get in life, and from the
shining smoothness of her whole face which,

instead of death, make you think of a dream
moving towards its climax and now and now
reaching fulfilment, and ultimately from her
half-naked—how did they use to put it? oh,
yes—ample bosom, which, in a kind of halluci-
nation, we imagine we can see moving up and
down.
No greater contrast imaginable between this
woman and this man: that between all alive
and quite dead. So then this woman there
actually opens her eyes—or is that still a
hallucination?—and shows that she's alive, first
just by looking and then by speaking as well,
not as if from a tomb but in casual, positively
bucolic tones. And even if she doesn't turn to
the man at her side, doesn't even have a peek at
him, it seems clear to whom she's talking:

My act now. Your act's over, Herr Krapp, Monsieur Krapp, Mister Krapp. Acted out under a false name in a language that wasn't yours. Well acted, of course, I give you that, with your affectation of a has-been, disillusioned clown. What was the point of dressing up in those oversized shoes? What was the point of all that fuss about munching bananas? Disillusioned? No. Not entirely. Right up to the end of your act and right up to the lights going out, your act still had the remnants of illusion. The remnants? A touch, a caress, a shimmer, a rhythm. They made your act a good act and your hopelessness not simply an old clown's routine—at moments it was inspired or, as I said, rhythmic. You sly old actor, Krapp. Or what should I call you? Krapp-of-my-heart?

Krapp the crocodile? Krapp-a-hard-act-to-
follow? Well it's my act now. And I haven't
assumed a false name, a stage name, neither
Effie nor Molly nor . . . I'm the one who's acting
and speaking, me, the woman beside you in the
almost motionless rudderless boat in the middle
of the flags of the nameless lake or pond
beneath a starry summer sky. And I'm speaking
and acting in my own language, my dear sir, the
language of my childhood and the language of
my senses. And I'm letting the past be. I'm not
listening to old spooools on the tape recorder,
I'm not reacting to my voice from decades ago.
What's past is present now—the summer, the
water, the boat, the flags, the stars, the silence.
And you? Not you. No trace of you. You did
perhaps play a role, but you're not playing a

role in my present, neither as a young man nor
an old one. Young, you? Summer in your life?
Never. We're acting out two different plays, my
dear boat-hirer. My act doesn't need a costume,
an arena, a cardboard nose, specially dirty
clothes. It doesn't need a slip on a banana skin,
machinery and props, doesn't need artificial
light and certainly not artificial darkness. My
act, in contrast to yours, doesn't need to be
articulated by pauses. If I speak without special
pauses, it's not because I'm a woman but rather
because those pauses—and above all yours,
those intentional, prearranged pauses of yours
full of hidden and yet completely unhidden
meanings—are not part of my act. Signs, yes—
but no meanings. Definitely no meaning! You
and your pauses for effect, Krapp. You and your

liturgies of pauses. You and your psalms of
pauses. You and . . . What would you be without that 'and . . .'? You performed every one of
your pauses. You composed them, like a com-
poser. The pauses never just happened to you
because of a dream, from sadness, from a fright.
My trust in you vanished, Krapp, whenever you
paused for thought, whenever you abused the
silence to pause for effect, Krapp, and every
time I silently begged: Don't do it again, Krapp.
And you did do it again, and again, Krapp.
Your unknown female on the other hand, me, I
can't pause for effect. I can't? I don't want to?
With your way of falling silent, you made it
impossible for silence to reign between us. With
your way of falling silent you were trying to
take charge of me, to impose your rule on me, a

despotic rule which would not be denied.
Despite that, I admit there were moments when
your silence did me good. Moments when your
silence woke me. Since it made me see reason.
Oh, moments when your silence made sure
there was quiet, quiet beyond meanings and
ulterior motives. A silence that set me thinking.
Thinking what? Thinking of what? Nothing but
thinking. Thinking with no ulterior motive. Real
bird became imaginary bird and vice versa.
Buddy Holly was singing 'Peggy Sue', even if no
one was singing and that silence alone reigned.
A stone opened its eyes. When he was a primary
school teacher, Wittgenstein, about to smack
one of his pupils, made sure all the child felt
was a slight draught . . . You made me believe in
that silence. Before you, the only silence I knew

was one that made me afraid. I had a horror of silence just as I had a horror of tiredness. You opened my ears for that silence, and subsequently my eyes. 'Just look at that quiet!' became our shared exclamation in that epoch, and it was an epoch, at least it was for me. During that epoch of open-your-eyes-to-the-quiet, the two of us used a form of the verb that doesn't exist in either of our grammars—the dual, the one that comes between the singular and the plural: 'the two of us heard, the two of us looked'. But at a particular moment I discovered that you didn't believe in that silence yourself at all, that silence that is great in such a different way from that of boundless space that sent a shudder of awe through Blaise Pascal, and not only him. Or this: you wanted to make

me, the other person, believe in it, but you yourself had no faith in the quiet world as the ulti-
mate ideal. You weren't the creator you would
have loved to be. You weren't at home in the
quiet world. The indescribable: you weren't
open enough, not permeable enough—not
enough of a shaper or, as I said, a creator, for it,
the indescribable, simply to appear without you
interfering and without you adding things, one
thing after the other. You were incapable of
leaving the quiet world to get on with its work,
to act out its own act, of leaving it alone, to put
it briefly. Instead you pointed at it, you, in the
first person: 'Look, now I'm showing this, and
now I'm showing this.' Instead of being a no
one in the silence, all the time you were the first
person, word by word, sentence by sentence. It's

not true that you had your doubts long after
that night in the boat among the quiet flags
beneath the silent stars—in the hour of your
death you had distinctly less doubt than back
then in the hour of our life. Back then, you
didn't let the world show itself at all. You didn't
believe in that eternity either—otherwise we
would have stayed together for ever, you and
me, not just in your words and sentences, after
the ball was over. And what a ball we had!
What a unity! But you weren't man enough for
that moment. You weren't child enough. You
never were a child, my dear sir. Though it's true
that a child, any child, constantly wants to
point something out, just as you do. Children
are always pointing, now in this direction, now
in that, and so on and so forth. Pointing and

wanting to point—that's even the most—how
shall I put it?—the most characteristic characteristic, the most pointed sign of a child that
is—how shall I put it?—on a level with its own
self. But what, you ask, does a child like that
actually want to point out? And my reply is:
nothing. At least nothing special, and above all
nothing significant. Children's pointing is not
intended, not meant to signify anything. A child
is sitting on the grass somewhere, stretches out
its arm, sticks out its index finger and points.
What is it pointing at? What is it indicating?
Nothing, absolutely nothing, not a thing, not
even the place, not even the wind, not even a
cloud. Nor even its outstretched arm, nor even
its own finger sticking out. A child doesn't point
out how it's pointing. It doesn't point out that

it's pointing. And when a child is pointing like
that, it's not pointing out anything to anyone
else, neither to its father nor to its mother nor
to another child nor to some stranger passing
by—or perhaps it is? Does it stretch out its arm,
does it stick out its index finger to point out its
three-times-nothing to a stranger? To an invisi-
ble person? Only yesterday, or whenever it was,
I saw a bus full of children drive past and one
of the children in it was just raising its arm and
pointing. At something outside? At the sky? At
me? At another bus? No, at nothing, nothing at
all, as if its arm were being hoisted by the
power of the nothing-at-all around the child,
activated by the pure joy of pointing at nothing
at all, ordered by no one, with reference to no
one. And no one, no other child on the bus,

PETER HANDKE

actually looked in the direction the child was
pointing. For there wasn't a direction and no
one, no other child, noticed that the child was
pointing. Perhaps the child itself wasn't even
aware that it was pointing. And all the time it
was uttering sounds into the bargain, decidedly
meaningless sounds, was playing with the
sounds. Playing what? Everything and nothing.
And you? And you? From the very beginning all
your pointing was meant to have meaning. And
all your sounds and then your sentences were
models on a catwalk which was supposed in
your intention to signify the world, and every
time it was the same model, with just a slight
change of dress, once in a sandbag, once in
ashes, once playing musical chairs. Did you not
tell me yourself that even as a child you had a

struggle with your constant being-aware, constantly being aware gave you problems, aware
of being, aware of existing, aware of walking
and of moving your arms to and fro as you
walked, aware of the position of your lips on
your face, aware of the back of your head and
above all aware of pointing to yourself for
others, one way or the other, and, even worse,
of having to have something to point out and
not just anything but something characteristic,
the something behind the something, the idea of
something—its sense or, as the case may be, its
non-sense, which, once you'd grown up, became
your speciality and later on, contrary to your
intention, the basis of your business, if you
don't mind my saying so? Awareness never
made a fool of you. Or perhaps it did—the king

PETER HANDKE

of fools, the senior fool. You were neither a
child of your parents nor a child of God nor a
child at all. Worse than little Jesus, who made
his mother and foster father spend three days
looking for him before they finally found him in
the temple of Jerusalem, where he had shown
himself more learned than the learned doctors,
you, even as a tiny tot, when you could just
about stand up, wobbling on your two little
legs, you erected your own temple around you,
the 'Temple of Neverending Interpretation and
Signification', in which, even as an infant piss-
ing and shitting in your nappies, you locked
away those around you in your I'll-show-you
prison, as you did me, the unknown female,
later on. Didn't your own mother go around
telling everyone that even the cry you gave

18

when being born was not at all the cry of a
new-born babe but echoed as if it came from
inside a sepulchre? So you gave your parents a
fright on your very first day on earth and there-
after everyone else, especially the children of
your own age. They approached you, attracted
by your 'angel face'—to use your mother's
expression—and as soon as you raised your
voice, they fled. Moreover your angel face fired
off the black looks of a Jeremiah at everyone
you saw, first of all from your cradle, then from
your tricycle, your bicycle, your horse, your
desk, from the top of your apple trees, from
high up on your ladder, finally from your hospi-
tal beds and, last of all, from your deathbed.
And what was your prophecy, from the cradle
to the grave, from A to Z? Our mothers give

birth to us between their outspread legs over an
open grave, then life as the glimmer of a brief
moment—the glimmer of a white stallion
through the gap in a barn—and immediately
afterwards the tumble into the sepulchre and
that was it. And in that brief moment? A drop
of milk, a drop of beer, a first and a last love,
and in the flags of a nameless lake a sigh up to
the stars, a sigh, a voice, which for once was not
speaking in sepulchral tones at all. And what
was the sound of that sigh? An 'Ah!' as at the
beginning of a play? An 'Oh', as at the end of a
play? Doesn't matter. What did matter—I
wasn't included in your sigh, you were sighing
for yourself alone. You were incapable of a duo-
logue. You were incapable of togetherness. In a
duo you were out of place and you sounded out

of tune. You only existed solo. Only in solitary seclusion did you think what you said and said what you thought and gave your true sighs. With others, with another person—out of your element. Solo—back in your element. Only solo did you move with your own body, laugh your genuine laugh. And that was how you were when you met me—a solo performer. You believed you were alone and, although you didn't move, you seemed to be dancing. And when you saw me, you lost your centre on the spot and that was the end of the dancing. I was going to turn on my heel, but by then it was too late . . . During all those years, whenever I was afraid of losing faith—let's not mention love and, especially hope—I left you to your own devices, even if only as a pretence—in reality to spy on you. Every time, thinking you were alone with yourself, you became a dancer again, whether in motion or motionless. An ambiguous dancer, one has to add—your solo dance was both serene and resigned, your steps, whether visible or not, both masterful and lost, your beaming both peaceful and warlike, your triumphant jubilation that of an idiot abandoned by each and every one. How easy it was to spy on you. Hardly were you on your own than I, the other person, ceased to exist. Even if I'd been spying on you right in front of your nose, only a few inches away, I wouldn't have been there as far as you were concerned. At one such time, when I drew attention to myself you started and ducked, as if I were a stranger who'd forced her way in, as if I were an enemy about to attack you. Still, by spying on you like that I saw you as the child you never were. Or no—it wasn't as a child that I saw you but as an orphan, an orphan at the moment of conception, in your mother's womb. Yes, decades after you were born you appeared to me in your mother's womb, the way she never saw you—a foetus in the form of a tiny, hunched-up old man, your face clearly defined and with a clear expression on it: 'I don't want to see the light of day! Existence is that last thing I want. Keep away from me, all of you, above all you and you and you.' And at the same time you were beaming, down there in your mother's womb. You acted out your 'No! No! A thousand times no!' with greater clarity and, yes, with more life than any other foetus could have

done. And so it stayed with you after you—
allegedly with a sullen old man's face—had
seen the light of day. Your consummate sullen-
ness caused general merriment among the rest
of us. Your doleful countenance, your constant
negativity were just as constantly mixed up
with a mischievous, magnificently pointless *joie
de vivre*. Your extra-gloominess was a power
station that generated extra light. Your act,
wasn't it seeking out—as an act—the others,
the rest of us, me? No, no, a thousand times no.
But from when you made your debut—yes, it
was a debut, yes, a thousand times yes—you
sent out signs. You yourself wanted to be the
embodiment of the sign. And a sign, my dear,
isn't that something that's directed at another
person, at other people? From your debut and

so on until the end of your days you, the
orphan, were sending out signs. And your signs,
worked out and acted out with such enjoyment
and rhythm, kept everyone else in their place
and created an insuperable vacuum around
you. You, the orphaned child, putting me in my
place as an orphan. My place was exclusively
in your sentences, in your 'boat', in your 'flags',
in your 'silence' and not with you, in you, for
one real second. And your sentences were never
questions. You never gave a sign that you
wanted me to question you. Your sentences
were unquestioned. And part of that was that
they were always witty. 'What's so funny about
that?' was your standing comment on other
people's sentences. If they weren't dressed up as
a joke, you refused to rank them as signs.

Arabic, you once said, has the same word for
'joke' as for 'dot' and to elevate a sentence, a
problem, a problem sentence, to the rank of a
joke was the final touch, like dotting the i, no,
as in Arabic, putting the dot *under* the i. Only
once, back then, now, in the flags—at last, no
more talk of jokes. And so the two of us stayed
together, inseparable. Back then, in the boat,
you finally let me be, let me have my share of
the night, let me have my centre. Till death us
do part? No, till day us do part. The day that
will part us—never will it come. Never will day
break in such a way within me and between us.
By leaving me in my dark night, you were a
good man for me, the unknown woman, just as
a woman once said in a Western, 'A good man
made me his wife, and I'm proud of that.' A

good man? For me, at least. For the dark,
gloom-ridden person was, perhaps is me, me,
the woman here. My act now? No, in my night
I never needed to act. You, you're the master
actor, world champion at broad-daylight acting.
No one can compete with you in that, no one,
never. But I can be your audience. 'I can put up
with being ignored,' another woman once said
to another man. Accordingly I join you in my
signless night, stammer vaguely to myself and at
the same time I feel the urge to sing my stam-
mering, the refrain to the song you're humming
of the shadow creeping down our mountains, of
the the azure sky growing dull, of the noise
ebbing from the countryside around us, of our
sleep in the coming peace. And I'm singing my
stammered echo now, singing my joyful anger

as a treble clef, just as you're singing your
serene lack of illusion. I wonder if that adds up
to a duet? No, or at least only if it's staggered
and in two different places, you in yours of
worldwide significance. And me? Oh, if only I
knew. Just moving my lips, the way under our
boat, under us all moved, and moved us, gently,
up and down, and from side to side. A continuing storm. Orion over the dunes of the Baltic.
No, no names. I'll say the name of Allah and
everything will be all right? I'll say the name of
Krapp and nothing will be right. A night without names. The star above the dunes, like that!
You rescued me. Rescuing as your way of
loving. That's the only way you can fall in love,
freely adapted from your foreign language. It's
only as a woman you've rescued that I'm in

your sight, for a while, just as we look at anything we've just managed to rescue, wide-eyed,
for a while. It's only as a rescuer that you can be
the man in the flags. A bus. A night. Waking up
with my head on a stranger's shoulder. Then the
stranger's head on my shoulder. Or is that
before? No, neither before nor after. The grass
behind the church. My heart has changed position, and you comment, 'In Arabic *to change
position* and *heart* have the same root.' Even
stranger. So strange that I entrust myself to your
care, still. Yes, in the flags there, in the boat
there, in the bus we were immortal, we are
immortal. No, it wasn't us who were immortal,
what was immortal was the lying there, the
being there, the having been there, the having
lain there. The hotel at the bus station. The

towels with AUTOESTACION on them, in capi-
tals. All night through the smell of snow, and in
the morning—*nada*. The sand in my shoes,
bought in the sale for a whole—no, no figures. I
am naked and you will clothe me. 'What mys-
tery! What beauty!' Ingrid Bergman says at the
end of her affair on the volcano, Stromboli. In a
shower of ash, in equilibrium. And out in the
courtyard the crackle of the buses parked
overnight. And the clinking of the bottles in the
minibar—no, no minibar. And the rustling of
the night wind in the curtain—no, no curtain,
or if there is, a plastic one, heavy, immovable.
And the cry of the owls in the middle of the
town?—Yes, in the middle of the town. And the
child crying in the next room, all night through,
quietly, very quietly—or is it just a noise in the

water pipes? And the roaring of the Mississippi.
And the clarity of the darkness, the geometry of
black. Impossible to stop listening. Impossible
to stop looking, you said, for me, in my language just for once— '*Niemals aus dem
Schauen herauskommen*.' And then? And then?
No then. And now? And now? A continuing
storm. 'You are my ruin, but perhaps there's
worse,' I say to that. Or, in your language:
'Helpless, helpless.' And now a pause from me.
No, holding my breath. Holding my breath
until my last echo on your last tape dies away.
Will die away. Will have died away. You never
expected anything like a riposte from me. No,
not even an echo. Not even a sound. You were
the sound and I resounded.

PETER HANDKE

What we saw at the end: She gradually with-
drew into her niche and, once there, closed her
eyes, just as gradually, her face and body as
ever bursting with life. Is it another hallucina-
tion that the male figure beside her appears to
be becoming like her, even if almost impercep-
tibly? Or is that merely a question of light (and
shade)?

October 2008

BIS DASS DER TAG EUCH SCHEIDET
ODER EINE FRAGE DES LICHTS

Was sehe ich da? Sieht das dort nicht aus wie
ein Grabmal für die römischen Ehepaare einst-
mals, Mann und Frau nebeneinander wie aus
dem Stein gehauen—nur sind das nicht bloß die
beiden Köpfe, sondern ganze Figuren, ein Paar
zudem wie in Lebensgröße, und losgelöst von
dem gemeinsamen Stein, oder was das ist—
keine Reliefs, sondern vollständige Skulpturen
oder Figuren, eine jede aufrecht in ihrer Nische
eng beieinander, wenn auch ganz und gar nicht
monumental. Gewand und Gesichter zeigen das
gleiche Grauweiß wie das sie umgebende
Steinhäuschen, oder was es ist. Grauweiß auch
die Augen, hier wie dort geschloßen. Beide
Statuen oder Gestalten stehen in derselben
Haltung, die Köpfe gleichermaßen geradeaus
gerichtet. Und doch springt uns bei längerem

PETER HANDKE

Hinsehen ein Unterschied zwischen den zweien
da dort an, über den üblichen zwischen Mann
und Frau hinaus. Der Mann, obwohl ebenso
aufrecht wie neben ihm die Frau, wirkt, mit
nicht nur eingefallenen und geschrumpelten
Wangen, sondern auch ebensolchem Mund, und
dazu den stark konkaven Schläfen, tot und
hinüber, wie man nur hinüber aussehen kann.
Daran ändert auch nichts, daß jemand, vielleicht
ein angeheiterter Passant, ihm die Lippen tiefrot
überschminkt, ihm eine rote Pappnase ange-
steckt und Bruchstücke wie von einem Tonband
um die Stirn gewickelt hat. Die Frauenstatue an
seiner Seite, trotz ihrer Kalkfarbe, erscheint uns,
wie sagte man einmal? als das blühende Leben.
Das rührt zuerst von ihren, wie eben nur im
Leben, zu einem hintersinnigen Lächeln

geschürzten Lippen, und überdies von der leuch-
tenden Glätte des ganzen Gesichts, welche statt
an den Tod an einen da auf seinen Höhepunkt
sich zubewegenden und sich jetzt und jetzt
erfüllenden Traum denken lassen, und zuletzt
auch von dem halbnackten Busen, dem, wie
sagte man einmal, schwellenden, den wir in
einer Art Halluzination meinen, sich auf und ab
bewegen zu sehen. Kein stärkerer Gegensatz
denkbar zwischen dieser Frau und diesem Mann:
der zwischen ganz Leben und ganz tot. Und so
schlägt diese Frau da dann auch in der Tat die
Augen auf, oder ist das weiterhin eine
Halluzination?, und zeigt sich lebendig, allein,
indem sie schaut, und nun auch spricht, nicht
wie aus einer Gruft, vielmehr leichthin und
nachgerade bukolisch. Und auch wenn sie sich

nicht an den Mann zu ihrer Seite wendet und
nicht einmal zu ihm hinäugt, scheint es klar, zu
wem sie da redet:

Mein Spiel jetzt. Dein Spiel, es ist gespielt,
Mister Krapp, Monsieur Krapp, Herr Krapp.
Gespielt unter einem falschen Namen, in einer
Sprache, welche nicht die deine war. Freilich,
zugegeben, gut gespielt, mitsamt deinem
Gehabe eines abgehalfterten, desillusionierten
Clowns. Was sollte die Verkleidung mit den
übergroßen Schuhen? Was sollte das Gehabe
mit dem Mampfen der Bananen? Desillusion-
iert? Nein. Nicht ganz und gar. Bis ans Ende
deines Spiels und bis zum Verlöschen des Lichts
ging von deinem Spiel der Rest einer Illusion

aus. Ein Rest? Ein Hauch, eine Brise, ein
Schimmer, ein Rhythmus. So war dein Spiel ein
gutes Spiel, und deine Hoffnungslosigkeit nicht
bloß Alte-Clown-Routine, vielmehr für
Augenblicke erleuchtet, oder, wie gesagt, rhyth-
misiert. Alter durchtriebener Spieler du, Krapp.
Oder wie dich nennen? Krapp-meines-Herzens?
Krapp, das Krokodil? Mit Krapp kein
Krippenspiel? Mein Spiel jetzt. Und für das
habe ich keinen falschen Namen angenommen,
keinen Bühnennamen, weder Effi, noch Molly,
noch . . . Ich bin es, die spielt und die spricht,
ich, die Frau neben dir in dem beinah bewe-
gungslosen, ruderlosen Boot mitten im Schilf
des namenlosen Sees oder Weihers unter dem
sommerlichen Sternenhimmel. Und ich spreche
und spiele, lieber Herr, in meiner eigenen

PETER HANDKE

Sprache, der Sprache meiner Kindheit und der
Sprache meiner Sinne. Und ich lasse das
Vergangene vergangen sein. Ich höre nicht die
Tooonbänder von einst an, ich reagiere nicht
auf meine Stimme vor Jahrzehnten. Was war, ist
jetzt—der Sommer, das Wasser, das Boot, das
Schilf, die Sterne, die Stille. Und du? Du nicht.
Von dir keine Spur. Du hast vielleicht agiert,
aber in meinem Jetzt agierst du nicht mehr,
weder als Junger noch als Alter. Jung, du?
Sommer in deinem Leben? Nie. Wir zwei
spielen zwei verschiedene Spiele, lieber
Mieter des Boots du. Mein Spiel braucht kein
Kostüm, keine Manege, keine Pappnase, keine
extradreckigen Gewänder. Es braucht kein
Ausrutschen auf Bananenschalen, keine
Apparate, Maschinen und Requisiten, kein

künstliches Licht, und schon gar keine
künstliche Dunkelheit. Mein Spiel, im
Gegensatz zu dem deinen, braucht nicht
skandiert zu werden von Pausen. Wenn ich
spreche ohne Extrapausen, so nicht etwa, weil
ich eine Frau bin, vielmehr weil die Pausen, und
vor allem die deinen, die vorsätzlichen, die vor-
gefaßten, deine Pausen voll versteckter und
doch gar nicht versteckter Bedeutungen, nicht
zu meinem Spiel gehören. Zeichen ja. Aber
keine Bedeutungen. Bloß keine Bedeutung!
Ach, du und deine Kunst-pausen, Krapp. Du
und deine Pausenliturgien. Du und deine
Pausenpsalmen. Du und . . . Was wärst du doch
gewesen ohne dieses Und . . . ? Du hast jede
deiner Pausen produziert. Du hast sie kompo-
niert, wie ein Komponist. Die Pausen, sie sind

dir nie unterlaufen, durch einen Traum, aus
Traurigkeit, vor Schreck. Wie habe ich jedesmal
das Vertrauen in dich verloren, sooft du deine
Sinn-Pausen gemacht hast, Krapp, sooft du die
Stille zu einer deiner Kunstpausen mißbraucht
hast, Krapp, und wie habe ich jedesmal im
stillen gefleht: Tu's nicht noch einmal, Krapp.
Und du tat's noch einmal, und noch einmal,
Krapp. Dein unknown female dagegen, ich,
kann keine Kunstpausen machen. Ich kann
nicht? Ich will nicht? Mit deiner Art von
Schweigen hast du verhindert, daß zwischen dir
und mir das Schweigen herrschte. Mit deiner
Art Schweigen wolltest du bestimmen über
mich, wolltest du mir dein Gesetz aufzwingen,
ein despotisches Gesetz, gegen das es keine
Widerrede gab. Trotzdem gab es, zugegeben,

Momente, da hat dein Schweigen mir gutgetan.
Momente, da dein Schweigen mich geweckt
hat. Da es mich zur Vernunft gebracht hat. Ah,
Momente, da dein Schweigen für Stille gesorgt
hat, jenseits der Bedeutungen und
Hintersinnigkeiten. Ein Schweigen, das mich
zum Denken brachte. Denken was? Denken an
was? Nichts als Denken. Sinnen statt
Hintersinn. Wirklicher Vogel wurde imaginärer,
und umgekehrt. Buddy Holly sang sein »Peggy
Sue«, auch wenn niemand sang und einzig jenes
Schweigen herrschte. Ein Stein machte die
Augen auf. Wittgenstein, dabei, als
Volksschullehrer einen seiner Schüler zu
ohrfeigen, sorgte bloß für einen leichten
Luftzug . . . Du hast mich an jenes Schweigen
glauben lassen. Vor dir kannte ich nur ein

Schweigen, das mir Angst gemacht hat. Es
graute mir vor dem Schweigen, so wie es mir
graute vor der Müdigkeit. Du hast mir die
Ohren geöffnet für jenes Schweigen, und in der
Folge auch die Augen. »Schau, was für eine
Stille!«, das ist unser gemeinsamer Satz gewor-
den in jener Epoche, und das war eine Epoche,
für mich jedenfalls. In jener Augen-auf-für-die-
Stille-Epoche herrschte, so bildete ich es mir
jedenfalls ein, zwischen uns zweien jene
Zeitform, die es in unser beider Grammatik gar
nicht gab: der Dual, die Zweizahl: »wir zwei
hörten, wir zwei schauten«. Aber in einem
bestimmten Moment habe ich entdeckt, daß du
selber gar nicht an jenes Schweigen glaubtest,
jenes Schweigen so anders groß als das der
unendlichen Räume, das nicht bloß Blaise

Pascal so erschaudern hat lassen. Oder so: Du
wolltest mich, die andere, daran glauben
machen, doch du selber, du hattest kein
Vertrauen in die stille Welt als der Weisheit
letzter Schluß. Du warst nicht der Schöpfer, der
du so gern gewesen wärst. Die stille Welt, sie
war nicht dein Vaterland. Das
Unbeschreibliche: Du warst nicht offen genug,
nicht durchlässig genug—nicht Gestalter oder
eben Schöpfer genug, daß es, das Unbeschreibliche, sich schlicht gezeigt hätte, ohne deine
Einmischung, und ohne deine Zusätze, einen
Zusatz nach dem andern. Du warst außer-
stande, die stille Welt ihre Arbeit tun und ihr
Spiel spielen zu lassen—sie, kurz gesagt, zu
lassen. Statt dessen hast du auf sie gezeigt, du,
in der ersten Person: »Achtung, jetzt zeige ich

das, und jetzt zeige ich das!« Statt ein Niemand
zu sein im Schweigen, warst du ständig die
erste Person, Wort für Wort, und Satz um Satz.
Es ist nicht wahr, daß du deine Zweifel hattest
lange nach jener Nachtstunde im Boot inmitten
des stillen Schilfs unter den schweigenden
Sternen: In der Stunde deines Todes hattest du
entschieden weniger Zweifel als damals in der
Stunde unser beider Leben. Da dort hast du die
Welt ganz und gar nicht sich zeigen lassen. Du
hast an jene Ewigkeit gleich nicht geglaubt—
sonst wären wir doch auf ewig zusammengeblieben, du und ich, und nicht bloß in deinen
Worten und Sätzen post festum. Ja, was für ein
Fest das war. Was für eine Einheit. Aber du
warst nicht Manns genug für jene Stunde.
Du warst nicht Kind genug. Du bist nie Kind

gewesen, lieber Herr. Wahr ist freilich, daß ein
Kind, ein jedes Kind, ohne Unterlaß etwas
zeigen möchte, wie du. Zeigen, zeigen tun die
Kinder, jetzt in die eine Richtung, jetzt in die
andere, undsofort, und so weiter. Zeigen und
zeigen wollen: Das ist sogar, wie soll ich es
sagen, das am stärksten bezeichnende Zeichen,
das am meisten handfeste Zeichen eines Kindes,
das, wie soll ich es sagen, auf der Höhe seiner
selbst ist. Was aber möchte so ein Kind, fragst
du, eigentlich zeigen? Und ich antworte dir:
Nichts. Jedenfalls nichts Besonderes, und vor
allem nichts Bedeutendes. Das Zeigen der
Kinder will und soll nichts bedeuten. Ein Kind
sitzt irgendwo im Gras, streckt seinen Arm aus,
spitzt seinen Zeigefinger und zeigt. Was zeigt
es? Was indiziert es? Nichts, rein gar nichts,

kein Ding, nicht einmal den Raum, nicht
einmal den Wind, nicht einmal eine Wolke. Und
auch den eigenen ausgestreckten Arm zeigt es
nicht, und auch nicht den eigenen gespitzten
Zeigefinger. Das Kind zeigt nicht, wie es zeigt.
Es zeigt nicht, daß es zeigt. Und wenn das Kind
so am Zeigen ist, zeigt es niemand anderem
etwas, weder seinem Vater, noch seiner Mutter,
noch einem anderen Kind, noch einem vorbei-
gehenden Fremden—oder vielleicht doch? Es
streckt den Arm aus, es spitzt den Zeigefinger
und zeigt sein Dreimal-Nichts einem Fremden?
Einem Unsichtbaren? Noch gestern, oder wann
das war, habe ich einen Autobus vorbeifahren
sehen, voll von Kindern, und eins der Kinder
drinnen war gerade dabei, seinen Arm zu heben
und zu zeigen. Auf was wohl draußen? Auf den

Himmel? Auf mich? Auf einen anderen Bus?
Nein, auf nichts, und auf wieder nichts, den
Arm wie emporgehievt von der Kraft des
Nichts-und-wieder-nichts im Umkreis des
Kindes, belebt von der reinen Lust, auf nichts
und noch einmal nichts zu zeigen, geheißen von
niemandem, bezogen auf niemanden. Und
wirklich hat ja niemand, kein anderes Kind in
dem Bus in die Richtung geschaut, in die das
Kind gezeigt hat. Denn es gab gar keine
Richtung, und niemand, kein anderes Kind hat
überhaupt bemerkt, daß das Kind gezeigt hat.
Ihm selber war vielleicht sein Zeigen gar nicht
bewußt. Und dazu hat das Kind in einem fort
Laute ausgestoßen, entschieden sinnlose, hat
mit diesen Lauten gespielt. Was gespielt? Alles
und nichts. Und du? Und du? All dein Zeigen

hat von Anfang an bedeuten wollen. Und alle
deine Laute und dann Sätze waren Mannequins
auf einem Laufsteg, der nach deinem Wollen die
Welt bedeuten sollte, und jedesmal wieder
dasselbe Mannequin, nur leicht umgekleidet,
einmal im Sandsack, einmal in Asche, einmal
als Bäumchen-wechsele-dich—nicht—und
nicht. Schon als ein Kind, hast du's mir nicht
selber erzählt, hattest du zu kämpfen mit
deinem ständigen Bewußt-Sein, hat es dir zu
schaffen gemacht, in einem fort bewußt zu sein,
bewußt, zu sein, bewußt, zu existieren, bewußt,
zu gehen und dabei die Arme auf und ab zu
bewegen, bewußt der Stellung der Lippen in
deinem Gesicht, bewußt deines Hinterkopfes,
und vor allem bewußt, dich den andern,
so oder so, zu zeigen, und, noch ärger, den

anderen ständig etwas zeigen zu sollen, und
zwar nicht gleich was, vielmehr etwas
Bezeichnendes, das Etwas hinter dem Etwas,
eine, die Idee von Etwas—seinen Sinn oder
sei es seinen Unsinn, was in deinen
Erwachsenen-jahren dann ja deine Spezialität
und später, gegen deine Absicht, mit Verlaub
deine Geschäftsgrundlage wurde. Das
Bewußtsein hat aus dir keinen Narren gemacht.
Oder doch: den König der Narren, den Narren-
Ältesten. Weder warst du ein Kind deiner
Eltern, noch ein Kind Gottes, noch Kind überhaupt. Ärger als der kleine Jesus, der von
Mutter und Ziehvater drei Tage lang sich
suchen ließ, bis sie ihn endlich fanden im
Tempel von Jerusalem, wo er sich schriftgelehrter
als alle Schriftgelehrten zeigte, hast du schon als

Winzling, als du dich gerade erst schwankend
auf den zwei Beinchen halten konntest, um dich
herum deinen eigenen Tempel errichtet, den
»Tempel des Nichtendenwollenden Deutens
und Bedeutens«, in welchen du als Säugling
schon, in deine Windeln pissend und scheißend,
deine Umgebung eingesperrt hast, in dein Ich-
zeige-euch-Gefängnis, wie später dann auch
mich, das unknown female. Hat nicht deine
eigene Mutter überall herumerzählt, daß schon
der Schrei, den du ausgestoßen hast bei deiner
Geburt, ganz und gar nicht der Schrei eines
Neugeborenen war, sondern einer, der schallte
wie aus dem Innern eines Grabs? So hast du
deine Eltern schon an deinem ersten Tag auf
Erden erschreckt, und in der Folge alle andern,
und insbesondere die Kinder deines Alters. Sie

haben sich dir genähert, angezogen—Ausdruck
deiner Mutter—von deinem »Engelsgesicht«,
und sowie du deine Stimme erhoben hast, sind
sie geflüchtet. Zudem hast du aus deinem
Engelsgesicht auf jeden und auf alles, was dir
unter die Augen kam, die finsteren Blicke eines
Unglückspropheten abgeschossen, zuerst aus der
Wiege heraus, und später von deinem Dreirad,
deinem Fahrrad, deinem Pferd, deinem
Arbeitstisch, aus der Krone deiner Apfelbäume,
hoch oben von deiner Leiter, zuletzt von deinen
Spitalsbetten, und ganz zuletzt von deinem
Totenbett. Und was war deine Prophetie, von
der Wiege bis zum Grabe, von Alpha bis
Omega?: Unsere Mütter, sie gebären uns zwi-
schen ihren gespreizten Mutterbeinen über
einem offenen Grab, das Leben als der

Schimmer eines kurzen Augenblicks—der
Schimmer eines weißen Rosses, der durch den
Spalt einer Scheune fällt—, und gleich darauf
der Plumps ins Grab, und das war alles. Und in
dem kurzen Augenblick? Ein Schluck Milch, ein
Schluck Bier, eine erste und eine letzte Liebe,
und im Schilf eines namenlosen Sees ein Seufzen
hinauf zu den Sternen, ein Seufzen, eine Stimme,
die einmal ganz und gar keine Grabesstimme
war. Und was war der Laut jenes Seufzens? Ein
»Ah!« wie zu Beginn eines Stücks? Ein »Ach«
wie am Ende eines Stücks? Egal. Was zählte: Ich
war nicht gemeint von deinem Seufzer, du
seufztest für dich allein. Du warst nicht fähig zu
einem Zwiegespräch. Du warst nicht fähig zur
Zweisamkeit. Zu zweit warst du falsch, und
klangst du falsch. Nur allein hast du existiert.

Nur in der Heimlichkeit dachtest du, was du
sagtest, und sagtest, was du dachtest, und ließest
die wahren Seufzer hören. Mit den andern, mit
dem andern: außerhalb deines Elements. Allein:
zurück in deinem Element. Nur allein bewegtest
du dich mit deinem eigenen Körper, lachtest du
dein echtes Lachen. Nur allein hattest du ein
Zentrum. Und so, als ein Alleiniger, bist du mir
ja auch begegnet. Du glaubtest dich allein, und
obwohl du dich nicht bewegtest, schienst du zu
tanzen. Und als du mich sahst, hast du auf der
Stelle das Zentrum verloren, und es war aus mit
dem Tanz, und ich wollte auf dem Absatz
umdrehen, aber da war es schon zu spät . . .
Während all der Jahre, sooft ich fürchtete, den
Glauben zu verlieren—von Liebe und insbesondere Hoffnung laß uns hier schweigen—, habe

ich dich allein gelassen, wenn auch nur zum
Schein—in Wirklichkeit, um dich auszuspähen.
Vermeintlich allein mit dir selber, wurdest du
jedesmal wieder, ob bewegt oder unbewegt, zum
Tänzer. Ein widersprüchlicher Tänzer, muß man
dazusagen: Dein Alleintanz war heiter und
zugleich resigniert, deine Schritte, ob sichtbar
oder nicht, eroberungslustig und zugleich verloren, dein Strahlen friedlich und zugleich kriege-
risch, dein Triumphieren das eines von allem
und jedem verlassenen Idioten. Wie leicht war
es, dich auszuspähen. Kaum warst du allein, gab
es mich, die andere, augenblicks nicht mehr.
Selbst wenn ich dich ausgespäht hätte dicht vor
deinem Gesicht, eine Handbreite davor, wäre
ich für dich nicht vorhanden gewesen. Als ich
mich so einmal bemerkbar gemacht habe, bist

du zusammengefahren und hast dich wegge-
duckt vor mir wie vor einem fremden Ein-dring-
ling, wie vor einem feindlichen Angriff.
Immerhin, indem ich dich so ausgespäht habe,
bist du mir erschienen als das Kind, das du nie
gewesen bist. Oder nein: Nicht als ein Kind
habe ich dich so gesehen, sondern als eine
Waise, eine Waise schon im Moment der
Empfängnis, schon im Bauch seiner Mutter. Ja,
Jahrzehnte nach deiner Geburt bist du mir
erschienen im Bauch deiner Mutter, so wie diese
dich nie gesehen hat: ein Fötus in Gestalt eines
da zusammengekrümmten winzigen Alten, das
Gesicht klar gezeichnet, und mit dem klaren
Ausdruck: »Das Licht der Welt—ich will es
nicht sehen! Nur keine Existenz! Bleibt alle weg
von mir, und vor allem du, du, und du!« Und

zur gleichen Zeit, da unten, im Bauch deiner
Mutter, hast du gestrahlt. Dein »Nein! Nein!
Und abermals nein!«, du hast es schon gespielt,
entschieden klarer und, ja, lebendiger, als
irgendein anderer Fötus es hätte spielen können.
Und so ist es mit dir geblieben, nachdem du,
angeblich mit dem grämlichen Gesicht eines
Greises, das Licht der Welt erblickt hattest. Mit
deinem formvollendeten Gram hast du unserei-
nen angesteckt zu Heiterkeit. In deiner
Leichenbittermiene und in deinem steten
Verneinen hat ebenso stetig mitgespielt eine ver-
schmitzte, herrlich sinnlose Lebenslust. Dein
Extraschwarzsehen war ein Kraftwerk, das ein
Extralicht erzeugt hat. Dein Spiel, suchte es
nicht, als Spiel, gleichwohl die andern, unserei-
nen, mich? Nein, nein, und abermals nein. Doch

ab deinem Debut—ja, es war ein Debut, ja, und
abermals ja—schicktest du Zeichen aus. Du selber wolltest das verkörperte Zeichen sein. Und
ein Zeichen, nicht wahr, mein Lieber, das richtet
sich an den anderen, an die anderen. Du, das
Waisenkind, sandtest ab deinem Debut und so
weiter bis ans Ende Deiner Tage Zeichen aus.
Mit deinen so spielfreudig kombinierten und
rhythmisierten Zeichen hast du freilich die
andern alle auf ihre Plätze verwiesen und
einen unüberwindlichen Leerraum um dich
geschaffen. Du, der Verwaiste, mein Verwaiser.
Mein Platz war ausschließlich in deinen Sätzen,
in deinem »Boot«, in deinem »Schilf«, in
deinem »Schweigen«, und für keine einzige
Realse-kunde bei dir, in dir. Und deine Sätze
waren nie Fragen. Nie gabst du ein Zeichen,

daß du von mir gefragt werden wolltest. Deine
Sätze waren fraglos. Und dazu gehörte, daß sie
immer witzig waren. Wo ist da der Witz? so
deine stehende Wendung auf die Sätze der
anderen. Kamen sie nicht in Gestalt eines
Witzes, bekamen sie von dir nicht den Rang
eines Zeichens zugeschrieben. Im Arabischen,
sagtest du einmal, gebe es das gleiche Wort für
»Witz« und für »Tüpfelchen«, und einen Satz,
ein Problem, ein Satzproblem in den Rang eines
Witzes zu erheben, sei das Tüpfelchen auf?,
nein, wie eben im Arabischen, das Tüpfelchen
unter dem i. Nur einmal, damals, jetzt im
Schilf: Endlich keine Rede von Witzen mehr.
Und so sind wir beide zusammengeblieben,
unzertrennlich. Damals im Boot hast du mich
endlich gelassen, mir gelassen auch meinen Teil

von der Nacht, hast mir mein Zentrum gelassen.
Bis daß der Tod uns scheidet? Nein, bis daß der
Tag uns scheidet. Der Tag, der uns scheidet:
Nie wird er kommen. Nie wird es in mir und
zwischen uns auf solch eine Weise Tag werden.
Indem du mich in meiner dunklen Nacht gelassen hast, bist du für mich, die unbekannte Frau,
ein guter Mann gewesen, so wie im Western die
Frau einmal gesagt hat: »Ein guter Mann hat
mich zu seiner Frau genommen, und das ist
mein Stolz!« Ein guter Mann? Wenigstens für
mich. Denn der dunkle, der umdüsterte Mensch,
das war, das bin vielleicht ich, ich, die Frau hier.
Mein Spiel jetzt? Nein, in meiner Nacht hatte
ich es niemals nötig, zu spielen. Du, du bist der
Meister des Spiels, der Weltchampion des tag-
hellen Spiels. Niemand kann und darf sich

damit messen, *no one*, *never*. Aber ich kann und darf deine Zuschauerin sein. »Ich kann es ertragen, übergangen zu werden«, hat eine andere Frau einst einem anderen Mann bedeutet. Und dementsprechend schließe ich mich dir an in meiner zeichenlosen Nacht, stammle dunkel vor mich hin, und zugleich drängt es mich doch, mein Gestammel zu singen, den Refrain zu dem von dir gesummten Lied, vom Schatten, der an unseren Bergen herabsteigt, vom Azur des Himmels, das sich verhärtet, vom Lärm, der verebbt aus unsrer Landschaft, vom Schlaf im Frieden, der bevorsteht. Und mein gestammeltes Echo singe ich jetzt, als Notenschlüssel den fröhlichen Zorn, so wie du die heitere Illusionslosigkeit. Ob das ein Duett ergibt? Nein, oder höchstens zeitversetzt, und an zwei

verschiedenen Orten, du an deinem weltbedeu-
tenden, und ich? Ah, wenn ich das wüßte.
Nichts als die Lippen bewegen, so wie sich unter
unserem Boot, unter uns sich alles bewegt, und
uns mitbewegt, sanft, auf und nieder, hin und
her. Fortdauernder Sturm. Der Orion über den
Dünen der Baltischen See. Nein, keine Namen.
Nur keine Namen. Ich sage den Namen Allahs,
und alles wird gut? Ich sage den Namen Krapp,
und nichts geht mehr. Eine Nacht ohne Namen.
Der Stern oberhalb der Düne, so! Du hast mich
gerettet. Retten als deine Art Lieben. Nur so
kannst du in Liebe fallen, frei nach deiner
Fremdsprache. Nur als von dir Gerettete bin ich
in deinem Blick, eine Zeitlang, so wie man
eben alles gerade noch Gerettete anschaut, mit
großen Augen, eine Zeitlang. Nur als Retter

kannst du der Mann im Schilf sein. Ein Bus.
Eine Nacht. Aufwachen mit dem Kopf auf der
Schulter eines Fremden. Dann der Kopf des
Fremden auf der Schulter, der meinen. Oder ist
das vorher? Nein, weder Vorher noch Nachher.
Das Gras hinter der Kirche. Das Herz hat seine
Position gewechselt, und du dazu: »Im
Arabischen haben die Position wechseln und
Herz dieselbe Wurzel.« Seltsamer. So seltsam,
daß ich mich dir anvertraue, immer noch. Ja,
im Schilf dort, im Boot dort, im Bus dort waren
wir unsterblich, sind wir unsterblich. Nein,
nicht wir waren unsterblich, unsterblich war
das Daliegen, das Dasein, das Dagewesensein,
das Dagelegensein. Das Hotel im Busbahnhof.
Die Handtücher mit der Aufschrift AUTO-
ESTACION, in Großbuchstaben. Nachtlang der

Geruch nach Schnee, und am Morgen: nada.
Der Sand in meinen Schuhen, gekauft im
Schlußverkauf für ganze—nein, keine Zahlen.
Ich bin nackt, und du wirst mich bekleiden.
»Welch Geheimnis! Welche Schönheit!« sagt
Ingrid Bergman am Ende ihrer Geschichte auf
dem Vulkan Stromboli. Im Aschenregen im
Gleichgewicht. Und im Hof das Knistern der
über Nacht abgestellten Busse. Und das Klingeln
der Flaschen in der Minibar—nein, keine
Minibar. Und das Rascheln des Nachtwinds im
Vorhang—nein, kein Vorhang, und wenn, dann
einer aus Plastik, schwer, unbeweglich. Und die
Eulen-schreie, mitten in der Stadt?—ja, mitten
in der Stadt. Und das nachtlang weinende Kind
nebenan, leise, sehr leise—oder ist das bloß ein
Geräusch in den Wasserrohren? Und das

Röhren des Mississippi. Und die Klarheit der
Dunkelheit, die Geometrie des Schwarz.
Niemals aus dem Hören herauskommen.
»Niemals aus dem Schauen herauskommen!«
sagst du darauf, für mich, in meiner Sprache,
ausnahmsweise. Und dann? Und dann? Kein
dann. Und jetzt? Und jetzt? Fortdauernder
Sturm. »Du bist mein Untergang, aber es gibt
vielleicht Schlimmeres!« sage darauf ich. Oder,
in deiner Sprache: »Helpless, helpless.« Hilflos,
hilflos. Und jetzt eine Pause meinerseits? Nein,
ein Innehalten. Ein Innehalten, bis mein letztes
Echo auf dein letztes Band verhallt. Verhallen
wird. Verhallt sein wird. Etwas wie eine Replik
von mir hast du nie erwartet. Ja, nicht einmal
ein Echo. Nicht einmal einen Hall. Du der Hall,
und ich der Nachhall.

Was wir zuletzt noch gesehen haben: Sie ist all-
mählich zurück in ihre Nische getreten und hat
dort, ebenso allmählich, die Augen geschlossen,
Gesicht und Körper blühend wie eh und je. Ist
es nun wieder eine Halluzination, daß die
männliche Figur zu ihrer Seite sich der Frau
anzugleichen scheint, wenn auch kaum merk-
lich? Oder ist das bloß eine Frage des Lichts
(und des Schattens)?

Oktober 2008

JUSQU'À CE QUE LE JOUR VOUS SÉPARE

OU UNE QUESTION DE LUMIÈRE

Que voyons-nous là? Est-ce que cela ne ressemble pas à un tombeau pour les couples romains d'autrefois, homme et femme l'un à côté de l'autre comme taillés dans la pierre—seulement ce ne sont pas que les deux têtes qui sont en relief mais le corps entier, un couple grandeur nature, en même temps détaché de la pierre commune, pas en relief, mais pour ainsi dire, des sculptures ou figures entières, chacune debout dans sa niche serrée, l'une près de l'autre. Vêtements et visages montrent le même gris-blanc que l'alcôve qui les abrite. Gris-blanc aussi les yeux, ici comme là fermés. Les deux statues ou figures ont la même attitude, les têtes pareillement alignées.

Cependant en regardant plus longuement, une différence saute aux yeux, et bien plus grande

que celle entre homme et femme. L'homme,
bien que debout comme la femme à côté de lui,
semble, non seulement à cause de ses joues
creuses et ratatinées, mais aussi à cause de cette
bouche rétrécie et de ces tempes concaves, mort
et au-delà, comme seulement on peut paraître
au-delà. Ça ne change rien que quelqu'un,
peut-être un passant éméché, lui ait barbouillé
les lèvres en rouge, lui ai collé un nez de clown
rouge et embobiné le front de fragments d'une
bande magnétique.
La statue de la femme à ses côtés, malgré sa
couleur de craie, nous apparaît comme, com-
ment disait-on jadis? la vie fleurissante. Cela
provient d'abord, comme seulement dans la vie,
de ses lèvres retroussées et du large sourire
énigmatique qui s'y dessine, de l'éclat lumineux

qui irradie son visage, lequel au lieu de la mort
apparait comme dans un rêve qui se déploie
vers sa culmination, et enfin, de ses seins à
moitié nus qui, comment disait-on jadis? qui se
gonflent, et que l'on voit comme dans une sorte
d'hallucination aller et venir au rythme de sa
respiration.
Il n'existe pas de contraste plus grand entre cet
homme et cette femme: c'est le contraste entre
la mort et la vie. Et c'est à ce moment que les
yeux de la femme s'ouvrent, ou bien est-ce là
encore une hallucination? Non, elle se montre
vivante, d'abord seulement par son regard, puis
elle se met à parler avec une voix qui ne sort
pas du fond d'un caveau, mais qui a l'air plutôt
légère et presque bucolique. Et quand même
par moments tranchante. Et même si elle ne se

*tourne pas vers l'homme à ses côtés, ne le
regarde pas non plus, il est clair à qui elle
s'adresse*:

Mon jeu maintenant. Ton jeu est joué, Mister
Krapp, Monsieur Krapp. Joué sous un faux
nom, dans une langue qui n'était pas la tienne.
Mais, je l'admets, bien joué, avec tes aspects de
vieux clown désillusionné. Enfin, pas totale-
ment désillusionné. Jusqu'à la fin de ton jeu,
jusqu'à l'extinction de la lumière, jusqu'à la
tombée du rideau tu laissais émaner de ton jeu
un reste d'une illusion. Un reste? Un brin, une
brise, une lueur, un rythme. A cause de ça, ton
jeu était un bon jeu, ton désespoir pas seulement la routine d'un vieux clown, mais par

moments, illuminé—comme je disais: rythmé.
Vieux joueur rusé, Krapp, ou comment
t'appeler: Krapp-de-mon cœur? Crapule-sans-
corps? Maintenant mon jeu. Et pour cela je n'ai
pas emprunté un faux nom, un nom de scène,
ni Effi, ni Molly, ni . . . C'est moi qui joue, c'est
moi qui parle, moi, la femme à côté de toi dans
le bateau presque immobile, sans rame, au
milieu des roseaux du lac ou de l'étang-sans-
nom sous un ciel étoilé d'été. Et je parle, je
joue, dans ma propre langue, Mister, la langue
de mon enfance et la langue de mes sens. Et
dans mon jeu, je ne parle pas du passé, je
n'écoute pas les bobines, bobiiines d'antan, je
ne réagis pas à ma voix enregistrée par moi-
même des décennies avant. Ce qui était, est
maintenant, et maintenant dans mon jeu agit

l'été, l'eau, le bateau, les roseaux, les étoiles, le silence. Et toi? Pas toi. Pas de traces de toi. Tu as peut-être agi, mais dans mon temps présent, tu n'agis plus, tu n'existes pas dans mon jeu, ni comme vieux ni comme jeune acteur—jeune? toi? jamais! jamais de ta vie c'était l'été !—, ni comme acteur tout court. Nous deux là, nous jouons deux jeux différents. Mon jeu n'est pas le tien, Monsieur-le-locataire-du-bateau. Mon jeu n'a pas besoin de costume de manège, de nez en carton rouge, de vêtements expressément crasseux, de chaussures franchement surdimensionnées, mon jeu n'a pas besoin de glisser sur les peaux de bananes, n'a pas besoin d'appareils, de machines, d'accessoires, de lumière artificielle, et surtout pas d'obscurité artificielle. Et mon jeu, à l'opposé du tien n'a pas besoin

d'être scandé par des pauses. Je parle sans
pauses, non parce que je suis une femme, mais
parce que les pauses et surtout tes pauses à toi,
des pauses faites exprès; des pauses pleines de
significations cachées et finalement pas du tout
cachées, cela ne fait pas partie de mon jeu per-
sonnel, de mon jeu à moi. Et à l'opposé de toi,
je ne joue pas avec le silence. Ton silence, mon
seigneur, tes silences, étaient autrement bavards
que tes paroles, que mes paroles, que nos
paroles. Et en plus, avec ton silence, tu n'as
jamais fait régner entre nous deux le silence, tu
voulais régner avec ton silence (toi-même), sur
moi, l'autre. Avec tes silences, chaque fois, tu
voulais avoir raison, raison contre moi, raison
de moi. Ton silence, chaque fois, quand tu l'as
fait surgir dans ton jeu, a imposé la loi entre toi

et moi—non, pas la loi—ta loi à toi—une loi
despotique, contre laquelle il n'y avait pas de
recours possible. II existait quand même des
moments, je dois l'avouer, où le silence que tu
as imposé, m'a fait du bien. Des moments, où
ton silence m'a réveillée; où ton silence m'a
véritablement— raisonnée. Des moments, ah,
où ton silence a véritablement fait le silence, en
moi et en même temps autour de nous deux,
contrairement à la plupart de tes silences un
silence, ah, au-delà des mots et au-delà des
arrières-pensées, un silence qui m'a fait penser.
Penser quoi? Penser à quoi? Purement penser,
un silence qui était la pensée pure, immobilité
qui s'envolait, sans arrêt, sans arrêt, en restant
immobile et matériel, ah, comme il était
magnifique ce silence, ton silence, le nôtre,

magnifique. Oiseau réel devenait oiseau imaginaire, et à l'envers. Buddy Holly chantait sa »Peggy Sue« même si personne ne chantait et seulement ce silence régnait. Une pierre ouvrait ses yeux et nous regardait. Wittgenstein, en train de donner une gifle à un de ses élèves de l'école élémentaire remuait seulement l'élément air . . . Tu m'as fait croire à ce silence-là. Avant toi le silence tout court m'a fait peur. J'avais horreur du silence comme je détestais en analogie la fatigue. Tu m'as ouvert les oreilles pour ce silence inconnu et aussi les yeux. »Regarde, quel silence!«, c'est devenu notre phrase commune à l'époque, et c'était bel et bien une époque, pour moi en tous cas. Mais à un moment donné j'ai découvert que toi-même, tu ne croyais pas à ce silence-là, un silence autrement grand que celui de ces espaces infinis qui n'a pas seulement effrayé Blaise Pascal. Autrement dit: Tu voulais moi, l'autre, m'y faire croire, mais toi-même, tu n'avais pas confiance au monde silencieux comme l'ultime philosophie. Tu n'étais pas le créateur que tu as prétendu être. Le monde silencieux n'était pas ta patrie. L'indescriptible: tu n'étais pas assez créateur pour que le silence se montre, sans que tu t'y mêles et y ajoutes, et y ajoutes . . . Tu étais incapable de laisser le monde silencieux faire son travail et son jeu, de laisser tout court. Au lieu de laisser montrer, tu as montré toi, en première personne—»attention, je te montre ceci, je te montre cela!«—, au lieu de personne tu étais toujours la première personne, parole après parole, phrase après phrase. Pas vrai que

tu t'en doutais longtemps encore après cette
heure de nuit dans le bateau au milieu des
roseaux silencieux sous les étoiles silencieuses:
dans l'heure de ta mort tu t'en doutais clairement moins qu'à l'heure même. Tu n'as pas
laissé là le monde se montrer seul, tu ne croyais
pas à cette éternité —sinon, on serait resté éter-
nellement ensemble, toi et moi, et pas seulement dans tes paroles post festum—quelle fête
c'était! quelle union que seulement la mort phy-
sique pourrait séparer!—pas seulement dans tes
soupirs d'outre-tombe . . . Tu n'étais pas assez
homme pour ce moment, tu n'étais pas assez
enfant. Tu n'étais jamais enfant, mon seigneur.
C'est vrai: un enfant, il veut sans cesse montrer
aussi. Montrer, montrer, maintenant dans cette
direction, maintenant dans l'autre, et cetera et

cetera, cela est même le signe le plus signifiant, le plus palpable d'un enfant, qui est, comment dire, à la hauteur de lui-même. Mais qu'est-ce qu'il veut montrer cet enfant-là? Rien. En tous cas, rien de spécial et surtout rien de significatif. Un enfant est assis dans l'herbe quelque part, écarte un bras, pointe son index et montre. Que montre-t-il? Qu'indique-t-il? Rien, aucun objet, même pas l'espace, même pas le vent, même pas un nuage. Il ne montre même pas son bras et son index, ne montre pas, comme il montre. Et s'il montre comme ça l'enfant, il ne montre pas aux autres, ni à sa mère, ni à son père, ni à un autre enfant, ni à un étranger qui passe, ou peut-être quand-même: il écarte son bras, pointe son index et monte trois fois rien . . . Encore hier j'ai vu un

bus passer, plein d'enfants, et un de ces enfants
à la fenêtre qui a levé son bras en train de
montrer, vers quelque chose à l'extérieur? vers
le ciel? non, vers le vide, dans le vide, le bras
comme levé par la force du vide autour de
l'enfant, lié à l'envie de montrer, montrer, montrer, rien et deux fois rein, à personne. Et en
effet personne, aucun autre enfant dans le bus
n'a suivi la direction dans laquelle l'enfant a
pointé—car il n'y avait pas de direction—, et
aucun autre enfant n'a vu l'enfant montrer. Lui-
même peut-être n'était pas conscient qu'il était
en train de montrer. Et toi? Et toi? Et toi? Déjà
soi-disant enfant, tu étais à chaque moment
conscient, conscient d'être, conscient d'exister,
de voir et d'être vu, de te montrer aux autres et
devoir montrer aux autres quelque chose, et

pas n'importe laquelle, mais une chose signifi-
cative, la chose derrière la chose, l'idée de la
chose—son sens et surtout son non-sens, cette
dernière signification devenant à ton âge adulte
ta spécialité, le fonds de ton commerce. Tu
n'étais ni l'enfant de tes parents, ni enfant de
Dieu, ni enfant tout court. Pire que le petit
Jésus qui a dû être cherché par sa mère et son
père au temple en train de se montrer plus
savant que les savants, tu as créé déjà petit,
autour de toi à chaque pas, même quand tu
avais encore du mal à tenir sur tes deux jambes,
ton propre temple, le temple de la »signification
ininterrompue«, un temple, vers lequel déjà à
l'âge de nourrisson, chiant et pissant dans tes
couches, tu avais attiré ton entourage entier, un
temple qui est devenu une prison pour les

autres, d'après ce que m'a raconté ta mère, et
plus tard finalement une prison pour moi. Ta
mère m'a raconté en plus que le cri poussé par
toi à ta naissance n'était pas du tout le cri d'un
nouveau-né mais un cri qui sortait comme de la
profondeur d'un tombeau. Ainsi tu as effrayé
tes parents dès ton premier jour sur la terre et
ensuite tous les autres, et surtout les enfants de
ton âge. Ils s'approchaient pour jouer avec toi,
attiré par tes »traits angéliques«—expression
de ta mère—, et aussitôt que tu levais ta voix,
ils prenaient la fuite. Déjà nourrisson, non seulement, tu parlais avec une »Grabesstimme«,
comme disent les Allemands, mais de ton visage
d'ange tu lançais en plus à chacun de tes
proches des regards sombres d'un petit pro-
phète de malheur, d'abord de ton berceau, et au

cours de ta vie, de ton tricycle, de ton vélo, de
ton cheval, de ta table de travail, du haut de tes
pommiers, du haut de tes échelles, et des cimes
et des creux des vagues de la mer du Nord, de
la mer Caspienne, du Lake Michigan et du
Lake de Tegucigalpa et de tes lits d'hôpital et
finalement de ton lit de mort. Et ta prophétie,
du berceau jusqu'au tombeau, avec laquelle tu
as tyrannisé avec succès le monde entier—
comme elle était paradoxalement, d'après les
éloges de tes admirateurs, presque joyeuse et
pleine d'humour insulaire—, qu'est-ce-qu'elle
annonçait d'Alpha à Oméga? A peu près cela:
nous sommes mis au monde par nos mères au-
dessus d'un tombeau ouvert, sortant de jambes
maternelles écartées et après la lueur d'une
petite seconde, d'un court éclair: tombés dans

le tombeau, et plus rien. Et pendant le court
éclair? une gorgée de lait, une gorgée de bière,
un match de baby-foot, un premier et dernier
amour, et entre les roseaux d'un lac sans nom
un soupir d'une voix s'élevant d'un bateau
presque immobile vers les étoiles, ta voix, mon
seigneur du lac-là, une voix, une fois et la seule
fois pas la voix d'un tombeau. Et qu'est-ce-qu'il
laissait entendre ce soupir? Un »Ah!« comme
au début d'une pièce? Un »Ach« comme à la
fin d'une pièce? Je ne me sentais pas concernée
par ton soupir, tu soupirais à toi seul. Ta mère
m'a raconté en plus, que tu n'étais pas capable
de parler à deux, d'être deux. Ou tu sonnais
juste et tu étais »juste« au milieu de plusieurs,
ou seul. À deux tu sonnais faux, tu étais faux:
avec ta mère, avec ton père, avec un soi-disant

ami, avec ton soi-disant amour, avec ton soi-
disant—avec notre enfant. Et moi j'ai appris:
seulement seul tu existais, seulement comme
clandestin tu pensais ce que tu disais et tu disais
ce que tu pensais et tu soupirais des soupirs
véritables. Hors de ton élément avec les autres,
avec l'autre. Seul: ton élément retrouvé.
Seulement seul tu avançais avec ton propre
corps, tu riais ton propre rire. Seulement seul tu
incorporais un centre. Et ce centre, il rayonnait,
il envoyait des rayons dans toutes les direc-
tions, et même si tu ne bougeais pas, tu avais
l'air de danser. Et c'est comme ça que je t'ai vu
la première fois. Tu te croyais seul et je t'ai vu,
et c'est comme ça que je t'ai rencontré. Et
quand tu m'as vue, toi, tu as aussitôt perdu ton
centre et ton rayonnement, et je voulais faire

demi-tour, mais il était déjà trop tard ...

Pendant toutes ces années, dès que j'ai eu peur
de perdre la foi, je t'ai laissé seul mais unique-
ment pour t'épier. Et seul avec toi-même, ton
éternelle maladresse de clown abusé et surtout
ennuyeux a disparu comme dans un tour de
magie—une magie naturelle. En mouvement ou
immobile, à ta table ou sous les pommiers, tu
redevenais un danseur. Un danseur ambigu, il
faut le dire. Ta danse solitaire: gaie et en même
temps résignée, tes pas visibles ou invisibles,
conquérants et en même temps perdus, ton
rayonnement paisible et en même temps celui
d'un guerrier, d'un idiot, d'un fou—d'un fou
non seulement sans roi, mais d'un fou aban-
donné par tout et par tous, et cela dès ses ori-
gines, dès sa naissance. Comme il était facile de

t'épier: dès que tu te sentais seul, tu ne te ren-
dais plus du tout compte de l'autre. Même
quand je t'épiais en face de toi à une longueur
de bras de toi, je n'existais pas. Toi seul existais,
toi et l'espace. Et quand je me suis faite remar-
quer, tu as à chaque fois sursauté comme s'il
s'agissait de l'intrusion d'un étranger, de
l'attaque d'un ennemi. Déjà ta mère t'avait
épié. Et elle m'a raconté qu'elle t'avait vu, à la
différence de moi, avec un certain amusement.
Pour elle tu jouais à toi seul une fois l'enfant-
pape qui, en épluchant des pommes de terre
dans la cuisine de la ferme, donnait sa bénédic-
tion urbi et orbi, ou l'enfant-chef d'orchestre
qui, en faisant ses devoirs, dirigeait un concert
retransmis dans le monde entier, ou l'enfant
indien, qui, avec une plume de poule pleine de

crotte dans les cheveux, à lui seul et avec sa
seule apparition faisait fuir l'armée du Général
Custer ou n'importe quelle autre au Little Big
Horn, ou au Silver Bow Creek ou au Crazy
Women River. Mais moi, en t'épiant, je t'ai vu
comme ni ta mère ni ton père ni un ou une troisième ne t'avaient vu: je t'ai vu, en t'èpiant,
comme l'enfant que tu es, mais jamais été:
quelqu'un auquel même s'il se donnait avec les
autres l'air adulte—un éternel adulte à fuir!—et
jeune déjà vieux, j'ai voulu m'adresser en excla-
mant: »Bonjour, enfant! ça va, enfant? tu as
froid, mon enfant?« Ou peut-être je t'ai vu, pas
comme un enfant, mais un orphelin, un orphelin né, un orphelin déjà au moment de la
conception, un orphelin déjà dans le ventre de
ta mère, et je t'ai vu, des décennies plus tard,

dans le ventre, comme ta mère ne t'a jamais vu:
un fœtus en forme de minuscule vieillard
accroupi là, le visage déjà clairement dessiné, et
exprimant clairement: »Je ne veux pas être jeté
dans l'existence! Je ne veux pas voir la lumière
du monde! Restez écartés de moi tous les
autres! Stay away from me everybody! Je ne
veux pas voir le jour, et surtout pas ensemble
avec toi, ni avec toi, ni avec toi!« Je veux être le
dépeuplé! Mais en même temps, déjà là-bas, toi,
le fœtus, tu rayonnais. Ton Non! Non! Non!:
tu le jouais, nettement mieux et vivace que
n'importe quel autre fœtus n'aurait pu le jouer.
Ton jeu, ne cherchait-il pas, comme jeu, quand
même les autres, nous autres, moi? Non, et non,
et encore non! mais dès ton début—oui c'était
un début, comme au théâtre, oui et encore

oui— ton jeu était signifiant, déjà comme
embryon tu voulais, oui, tu voulais signifier, et
un signe, ça existe pour les autres, ou on ne
peut pas parler d'un signe, n'est-ce-pas, mon
chéri? Toi, le dépeuplé, tu faisais dès ton début
et ensuite jusqu'à la fin de tes jours des signes,
tu as cumulé et combiné et rythmé les signes
avec lesquels tu t'es adressé aux autres en les
fixant chacun à sa place et en créant autour de
toi un infranchissable vide, et, en première
ligne, pour moi, toi, le dépeuplé, mon
dépeupleur. Ma place était exclusivement dans
tes signes, dans ton »bateau«, tes »roseaux«,
ton »si-lence«, et pas une seule seconde réelle
près de toi, pour ne pas utiliser le signe »cœur«,
qui, comme le mot »enfant«, ne faisait pas
partie de ton vocabulaire ou, comme tu disais,

de »ton trésor«. Et néanmoins nous sommes
restés ensemble, inséparables toute la vie et aussi
après ta mort, Pourquoi? Parce que tu m'as
laissée, à l'opposé des hommes avant toi, ma
part de la nuit, tu m'as laissé mon centre, avec
tous tes signes ô combien lumineux tu as épar-
gné mon obscurité, tu n'as jamais touché à mes
rêves. Jusqu'à ce que la mort nous sépare? Non,
jusqu'à ce que le jour, la lumière du jour nous
sépare. La mort ne nous a pas séparés, et le jour
qui nous séparerait ne va jamais arriver. Jamais
il ne va faire jour en moi et entre nous deux de
cette manière-là. En me laissant dans ma nuit, en
me laissant dans mon obscurité tu étais un
homme bon —quand même, quand même, au
moins pour moi. Je n'avais pas besoin d'une
place dans ton soi-disant cœur, chéri, ma nuit

dans laquelle nous étions inséparables était et est une place infiniment plus vaste que tous les cœurs du monde. Mon jeu maintenant? Non, dans ma nuit je n'avais jamais besoin et je n'ai toujours pas besoin de jouer. Toi, tu étais le maître du jeu, le maître des signes, le champion mondial du jeu clair journalier, le rabat-joie le plus jouissif, le plus joyeux . . . Personne ne peut se mesurer avec ton jeu et tes signes, no one, never. Moi, je te rejoins dans ma nuit insigni-fiante, avec quelques bribes de mots obscurs mais qui me poussent doucement à les chanter, des mots vagabonds qui répondraient peut-être à cette chanson que tu as chantonnée une fois pour moi, moi installée dans le noir: »L'ombre descend de nos montagnes, / L'azur du ciel va se ternir. / Le bruit se tait dans nos campagnes. / En

paix bientôt tout va dormir . . .«—chanter,
répondre maintenant moi, du fond de mon rêve,
en remuant mes lèvres, comme jadis sous
notre bateau et sous nous, tout remuait, et nous
remuait, doucement, de haut en bas, et d'un côté
à l'autre: Toujours la tempête . . . Sur les hauts
de Hurlevent . . . L'Orion au-dessus des dunes de
la Baltique . . . Non, pas de noms . . . Une nuit
sans noms . . . Une étoile au-dessus de la dune . .
. Un bus nommé désir . . . Non, pas de noms . . .
Un bus . . . La nuit . . . La nuit nous a pris à la
nuque et nous a transportés à un autre endroit,
à l'endroit juste . . . Et enfin, une fois, une seule
fois je t'entendais parler avec la voix d'un enfant
. . . Je me suis endormie, quelque part entre
l'abondance et l'abandon . . . Réveillée la tête
sur l'épaule d'un étranger . . . Plus tard, la tête

de l'étranger sur mon épaule à moi . . . Ou plus
tôt? . . . Non, pas d'avant et pas d'après, pas de
moment, pas d'heure, pas de temps . . . L'herbe
derrière l'église . . . Le cœur a changé sa position
et tu m'as dit qu'en arabe »changer la position«
et »cœur« avaient la même racine . . . cœur,
changer la position, se diriger, s'adresser . . . La
nuit dans l'hôtel qui faisait partie du terminal de
bus . . . Les serviettes de la salle de bain impri-
mées avec les lettres AUTOESTACION, en
majuscules . . . Toute la nuit l'odeur de la première neige, et le matin: rien . . . Non, pas de
matin . . . Oui, le houx à baies rouges, quand-
même . . . mais pas à Noël, non, dans la
brume... Le sable dans mes chaussures, achetées
en solde pour . . . Non, pas de chiffres . . . Plus
jamais je ne voulais marcher sans sable dans

mes chaussures . . . J'étais nue, et tu m'as habillé
. . . Je t'arrachais tes habits, et plus je les arrachais, plus tu semblais habillé . . . Le silence se
transforma en nos corps, et nos corps se trans-
formaient en silence, et mes boucles d'oreilles te
réveillaient une deuxième fois, et un train sifflait
pour la troisième fois, et le coq chantait pour la
centième fois—non, pas de chiffres, même toi,
éternel compteur, tu avais arrêté de compter—,
et la nuit durait, et la nuit durait et la nuit durait
. . . Je t'étais le calme, je t'étais odeur, tu m'étais
le calme, tu m'étais odeur . . . *The roaring of the
Mississippi* . . . Et le crépitement des bus garés
dans la cour . . . Et le tintement des bouteilles
dans le mini bar . . . Non, il n'y avait pas de
mini bar . . . Et le bruissement du vent de nuit
dans le rideau . . . rideau, ou il était en plastique,
lourd, immobile . . . Et le cri du hibou en pleine

ville? Oui en pleine ville . . . Et l'enfant pleurant
à côté toute la nuit, doucement, très doucement,
presque inaudible, ou était-ce seulement un son
comme un gémissement éternel, dans les tuyaux?
. . . Et la clarté de cette obscurité . . . La géométrie
de ce noir-là . . . Impossible de se cogner quelque
part, ni à une chaise, le seul meuble dans note
chambre, ni à la porte, même pas au poste de
télévision absent . . . Mais on n'avait pas besoin
de bouger toute la nuit . . . Pas bouger . . .
Jamais arrêter d'écouter . . . Plus jamais arrêter
de regarder . . . Nie mehr aus dem Schauen
herauskommen! comme tu as dit . . . Und dann?
Et après? . . . Kein dann, pas d'après . . . Et maintenant? Et maintenant? Et maintenant? Und
jetzt? Und jetzt? . . . Storm still? Tempête
tranquille? Toujours tempête? . . .

Et qu'avons-nous encore vu? Peu à peu, elle est rentrée dans son alcôve tout en parlant, et a peu à peu fermé les yeux; visage et corps resplendissant comme jamais. Est-ce une nouvelle hallucination, que le personnage masculin à côté d'elle, se soit peu à peu rapproché des expressions de la femme, juste un peu, mais quand même? Ou cela vint-il de la parole? Ou n'était-ce pas plutôt une question de lumière? (et d'ombre)?

September 2007

Afterword

Till Day You Do Part—an answer to Beckett's
Krapp's Last Tape? An echo, rather. An echo,
now distant in both place and time, now quite
close to Mr Krapp, the solitary hero of Samuel
B's play. An echo, now weak and contradictory,
distorted, now loud, amplified, enlarged. That
is why I make so bold as to call this echo
monologue a drama, a very minor drama—just

as *Krapp's Last Tape* is a drama, a great one. With that play Beckett achieved absolute reduction, a necessary reduction of the theatre, by freeing himself of the remains of symbolism and opinions about existence in his other plays. *Krapp's Last Tape* perhaps embodies the end or the terminus of the theatre, as pure theatre. It is a primary, essential play. Is it possible that after Beckett there were only our secondary plays, for example, as an example, *Till Day You Do Part*. No more reduction is possible, no more zero space is possible—just traces of those who have lost their way, here the first to lose her way?

But perhaps we had to lose our way, in the interest of the stage, of the theatre? Just as I said to myself one day, 'I will lose my way with determination!?' Lost, are we? Or embarked. Lost and embarked? As Pascal said: 'We are embarked'. Are we?

'Echo', if I remember rightly, is also the name of a person in Greek mythology, a minor goddess or a nymph (of which it says in the dictionary: 'a lower-ranked goddess inhabiting the underwood') but definitely a woman, the voice of a woman.